To: Penelope

Believe in the MAGIC of FRIENDSHIP

Love ~ Mary and Peggy

Sprinkles
in Tangle Town

Written by
Peggy Scott

Illustrated by
Mary Stayner

Author Peggy Scott
Illustrator Mary Stayner, CZT

No part of this book may be reproduced, stored in a retrieval system, or transmitted by any means without written permission of the author.

ISBN: 979-8-218-40967-8

This book is printed on acid-free paper.

Copyright © 2024
All rights reserved
Printed in the United States of America

ZENNER PRESS

Dedicated to those who believe that the power of friendship, when it is sprinkled to others, is positively *magical!*

Sprinkles started to step out of the bakery, which also was where she lived. She adored her home, which was in the apartment above the shoppe. The cute little shoppe was in the shape of a muffin. Her parents, Cookie and Muff N. Baker, had owned the *Lovin' Oven Bakery Shoppe* ever since she could remember. She knew her name, Sprinkles, had been given because of her parents' passion for baking.

"Sprinkles, where are you going?" asked Cookie Baker, busy cutting more sugar cookies to pop into the oven.

"I'm taking an extra-large sugar cookie to Old Man Gruff. I put extra sprinkles on it, of course," Sprinkles giggled as she replied.

"I hope you aren't becoming a pest. Mr. Gruff likes his privacy, you know," warned Sprinkles' mother.

"I think Old Man Gruff is starting to like me. When I first started taking him my special big sugar cookie with extra sprinkles, he slammed the door in my face, so I left it on the chair by his front door. He doesn't slam the door at me anymore. And guess what! Old Man Gruff said, 'Hmph' to me last week. I think that is good, don't you?"

Without waiting for her mother to answer and with a sugar cookie safely wrapped and clutched in her hand, Sprinkles skipped outside, with her auburn pigtails bouncing. It was another sunshiny day in Tangle Town. The sun caught the multi-colored sparkles on Sprinkles' light pink tee top. With it she wore her Tinkerbell-styled skirt of different shades of pink and lavender. It was one of her favorite skirts because it *twirled* in such a *fun* way.

Sprinkles looked down the street of Tangle Town, smiling at the homes and stores that she saw, each one being *unique* and colorful.

There was no doubt in Sprinkles' mind that Tangle Town was the very best place on earth to live.

As she skipped down the street she passed by the *Book Nook* and waved to Paige Turner, the owner of the bookstore. Paige was busy displaying new books in her store window.

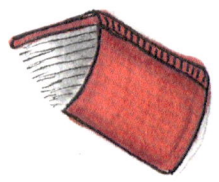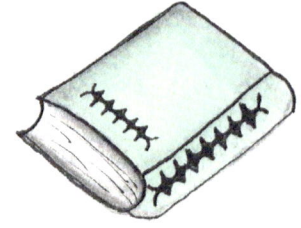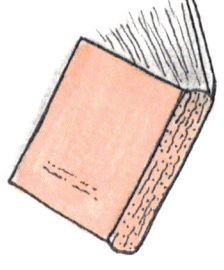

"Hello, Mrs. Budd," Sprinkles called to the florist as she skipped by the flower shop, *Rose's Bountiful Blossoms*. Sprinkles breathed deeply to capture the fragrance of flowers that lingered near the shop.

Sprinkles slowed down as she came to *Kitty Paws*, the pet shop. She always stopped to look through the big windows. She laughed at the antics of the furry little kittens, tumbling over one another as they played.

The people of Tangle Town all knew one another. They worked together. They played together. Everyone was kind. Well, almost everyone. Old Man Gruff lived on the edge of Tangle Town in an odd little house, which was painted plain old white. Old Man Gruff never smiled. Once a week he came to town to buy supplies. He grumped at the grocer. He snapped at the store owners, and he most certainly was never kind.

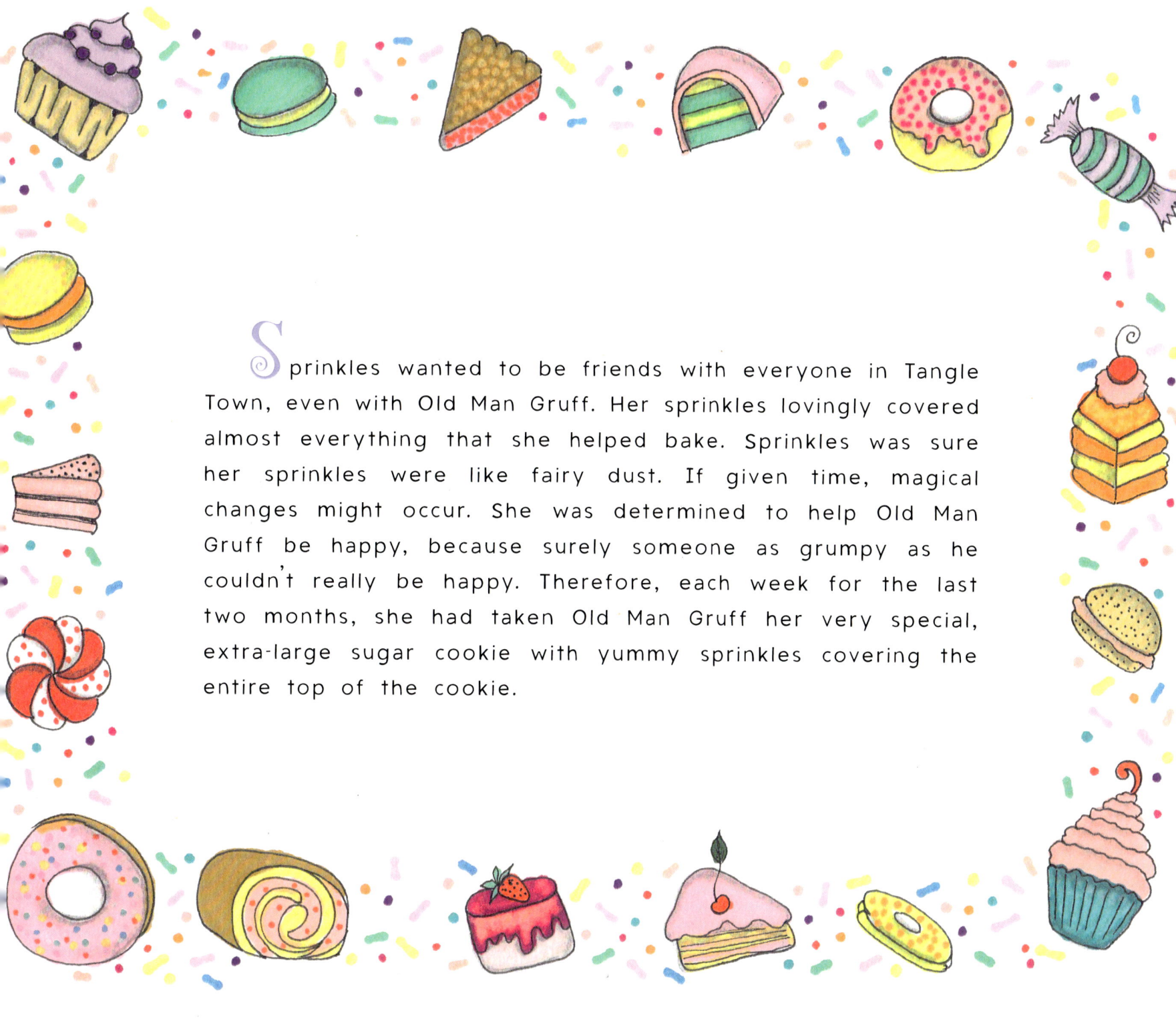

Sprinkles wanted to be friends with everyone in Tangle Town, even with Old Man Gruff. Her sprinkles lovingly covered almost everything that she helped bake. Sprinkles was sure her sprinkles were like fairy dust. If given time, magical changes might occur. She was determined to help Old Man Gruff be happy, because surely someone as grumpy as he couldn't really be happy. Therefore, each week for the last two months, she had taken Old Man Gruff her very special, extra-large sugar cookie with yummy sprinkles covering the entire top of the cookie.

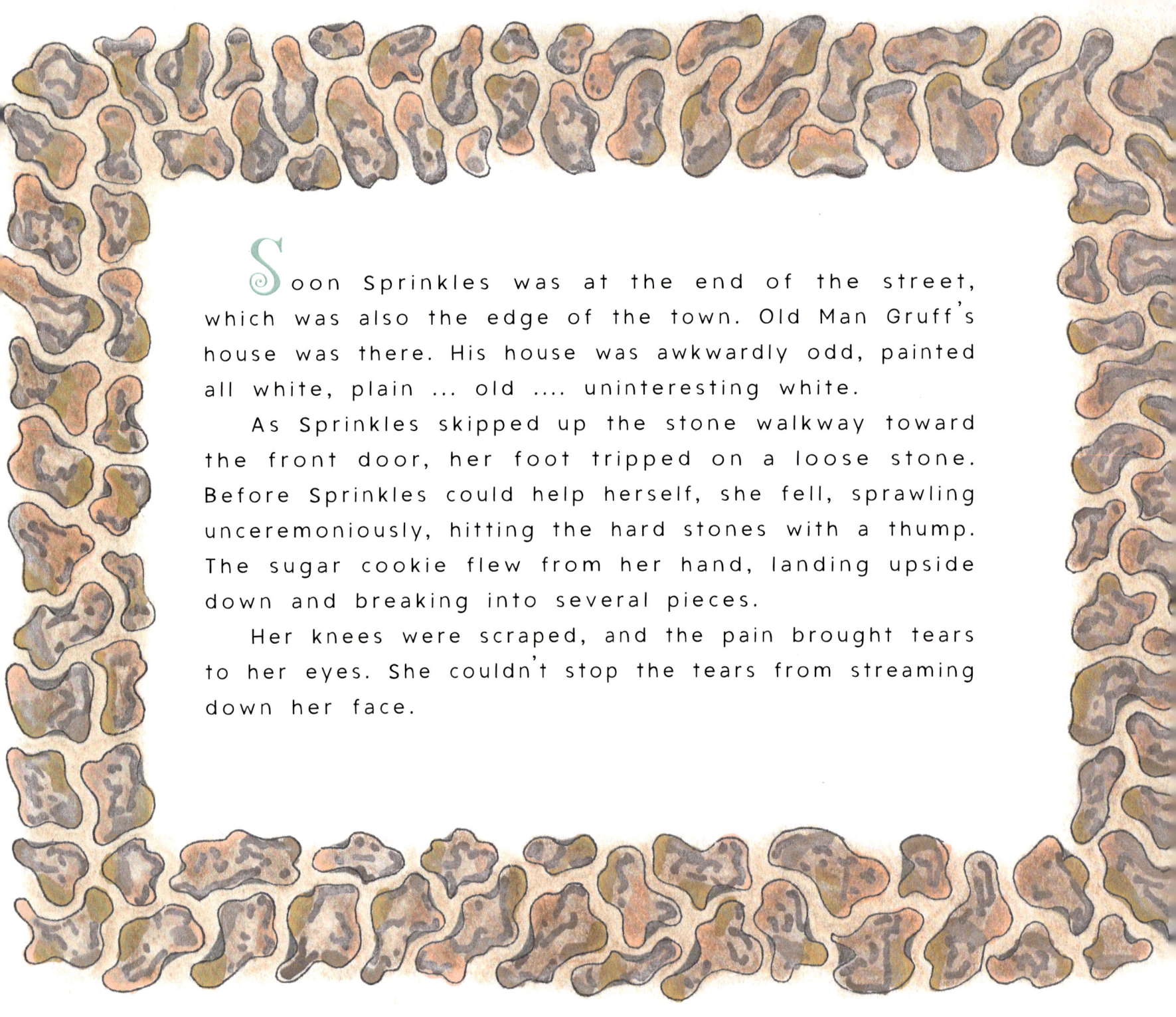

Soon Sprinkles was at the end of the street, which was also the edge of the town. Old Man Gruff's house was there. His house was awkwardly odd, painted all white, plain ... old .... uninteresting white.

As Sprinkles skipped up the stone walkway toward the front door, her foot tripped on a loose stone. Before Sprinkles could help herself, she fell, sprawling unceremoniously, hitting the hard stones with a thump. The sugar cookie flew from her hand, landing upside down and breaking into several pieces.

Her knees were scraped, and the pain brought tears to her eyes. She couldn't stop the tears from streaming down her face.

Suddenly Sprinkles felt gentle hands helping her up. Old Man Gruff carefully took her by her hand and helped her to sit in a chair on his front porch. Old Man Gruff looked at Sprinkles' scraped knees and in a quiet voice said, "I'll be right back."

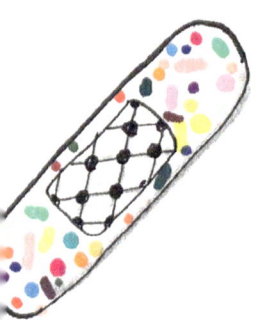

In a quick minute, Old Man Gruff returned with a soft damp cloth to clean Sprinkles' scrapes. He also carefully applied bandages to each of her knees. Sprinkles stopped crying, but for once, she wasn't sure what to do or say. Suddenly Old Man Gruff didn't seem so gruff. "I'm sorry that I dropped your cookie. I'm afraid it broke," Sprinkles whispered.

Sprinkles was surprised when Old Man Gruff sat down in the chair beside her. He looked at her with pale blue eyes that seemed sad and kind at the same time. "What is your name? Why have you been bringing me cookies each week?" he asked Sprinkles.

"My name is Sprinkles. Cookie and Muff N. Baker are my parents, and they own the *Lovin' Oven Bakery Shoppe* in Tangle Town. I help them when cookies or cupcakes or anything yummy needs sprinkles."

"I would say that Sprinkles is a good name for you," chuckled Old Man Gruff. "But that still does not explain why you have been bringing me a sugar cookie every week." Sprinkles was surprised to hear Old Man Gruff chuckle, but it was a nice sound and it helped Sprinkles to forget about her skinned knees.

"I think sprinkles are magical, just like fairy dust," Sprinkles explained. "You seem so unhappy. I always put extra sprinkles on your cookies hoping to make you happy. Why are you always so grumpy, anyway?"

For several minutes Old Man Gruff just looked down at the ground. Finally, he looked at Sprinkles and muttered, "I'm shy. I don't make friends easily. I haven't lived in Tangle Town very long, but long enough to know that my house is odd, different from all the other colorful and unique homes and stores in Tangle Town. I'm out of place in Tangle Town."

Sprinkles did not know what to say, so she thought it best to just listen. After a short pause, Old Man Gruff quietly continued. "Also, I have noticed that people's name in Tangle Town usually tells something about them. For example, Rose Budd owns the flower shop, *Rose's Bountiful Blossoms*, and Paige Turner owns the *Book Nook*, and so on. Even your parents, Cookie and Muff N. Baker own the *Lovin' Oven Bakery Shoppe*. My last name is Gruff and people seem to expect me to be like my name. Since I'm shy, it is just easier to be grumpy, so I don't have to talk to people. Most people don't really want to be around me. However, being grumpy is lonely. I don't know what to do to change."

Once again, Sprinkles didn't know what to say. Finally, after minutes of quiet thinking, she did what came natural to her. She reached out and gave Old Man Gruff a hug and the broken pieces of the sugar cookie.
"I'll be back," she promised as she walked slowly back down his stone walkway that led to the street of Tangle Town.

Sprinkles wasn't skipping. As she walked down the street of Tangle Town, her usual cheery greeting to her friends was gone. Everyone she passed noticed and everyone worried. What was wrong with Sprinkles? Her Tangle Town friends watched as Sprinkles slowly opened the door to the *Lovin' Oven Bakery Shoppe* and went inside.

Cookie looked up when the tinkly sound of the bell told her someone had just come into the bakery. She was immediately concerned when she saw Sprinkles. "My goodness! Why the unhappy face? What is wrong? Aren't you feeling well?" As a mother, Cookie couldn't wait for answers as she rushed over to Sprinkles and put her hand to Sprinkles' forehead to check for a fever. Then she noticed the bandages on both of Sprinkles' knees. "What happened to your knees?"

Sprinkles reached out and tightly hugged her mother as her tears started to flow. She wasn't crying because her knees hurt, but because her heart hurt for Mr. Gruff. She had decided she wasn't going to call him Old Man Gruff anymore. It just didn't seem right or very polite. As her mother comforted her, Sprinkles told the whole story of falling, how Mr. Gruff had helped her, and why Mr. Gruff acted so grumpy. "We must help him, Mom, but I don't know how. I don't think my taking him a sugar cookie once a week is enough."

The shoppe bell tinkled as Claude Hopper, still carrying a pair of new fuchsia tennis shoes that he had been unpacking for his shoe store, rushed into the shoppe. Rose Budd, Paige Turner, and Skye Blue followed close behind. They all looked concerned and started talking at the same time. "What's wrong with Sprinkles? Why is she sad? Is she sick? Is there something we can do to help?"

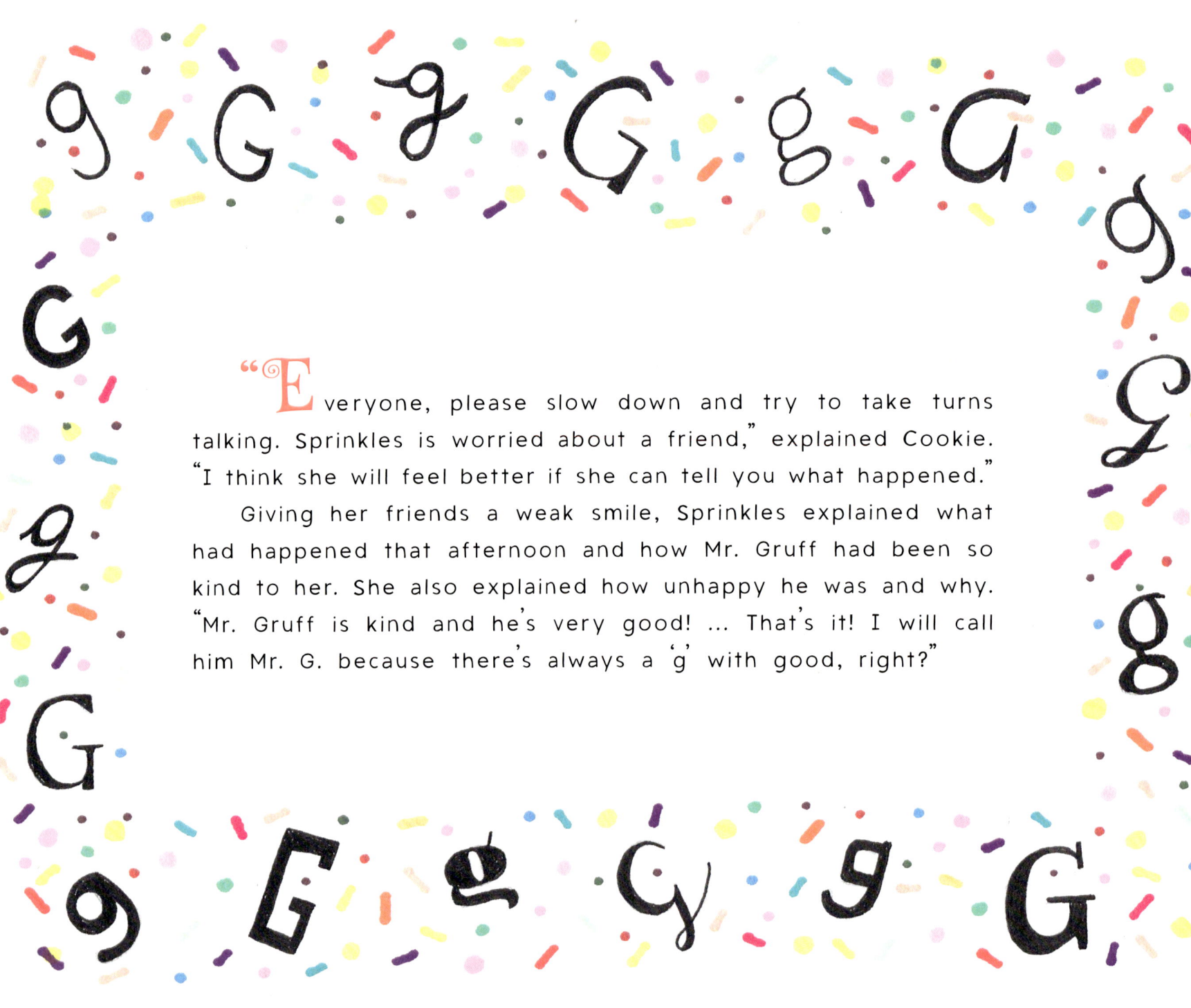

"Everyone, please slow down and try to take turns talking. Sprinkles is worried about a friend," explained Cookie. "I think she will feel better if she can tell you what happened."

Giving her friends a weak smile, Sprinkles explained what had happened that afternoon and how Mr. Gruff had been so kind to her. She also explained how unhappy he was and why. "Mr. Gruff is kind and he's very good! ... That's it! I will call him Mr. G. because there's always a 'g' with good, right?"

Sprinkles started twirling around and around singing,

"Mr. G. is good. Mr. G. is good. Mr. G. is good."

Sprinkles' mother and her friends started to laugh with relief as they watched Sprinkles. It seemed that she was once again happy and that a problem had just been solved.

Suddenly Sprinkles stopped and in a determined voice stated, "But that is not enough. We must do more to help Mr. G. feel like he is a part of Tangle Town, instead of feeling odd and left out. His house doesn't fit in with the rest of the houses in Tangle Town, and he knows it. We need to change his house." Again, Sprinkles started to twirl around the shoppe and this time she chanted,

"Change his house. Change his house. Change his house."

"Whoa! Slow down, Sprinkles. I think I have an idea," cried Skye with enthusiasm. Skye Blue, who owned the paint store, declared, "I'll supply beautiful bright-colored paints to repaint Mr. G.'s plain, white house."

Inspired by Skye's suggestion, Claude added, "I'll talk with my friend, Philip Tank, who owns the Gas Station. Philip has many types of tools and ladders that will be helpful. Philip also is very creative, and I imagine he can add special trims to the house so that it will no longer be so plain."

Not to be left out, Rose Budd chimed in, "When the house is trimmed and repainted, I will plant some rose bushes along his stone walkway."

"Speaking of the stone walkway, I have a book in my store called *Home Repairs*," reported Paige. "I think there is a section that describes how to secure loose stones in a walkway. We must fix the stone that tripped Sprinkles so that no one else falls."

Suddenly everyone was again talking at once and Sprinkles was again *twirling* around the shoppe. Everyone was happy to know they would be helping a neighbor of whom they looked forward to calling their friend.

It took almost a week to transform Mr. G.'s house. (Everyone in Tangle Town now knew Mr. Gruff as Mr. G.) During the time that friends and neighbors worked together to change the house, Mr. G. also began to change. Mr. G. became less shy as he realized he did not need to be grumpy to avoid talking with his new friends, because now he wanted to talk with them.

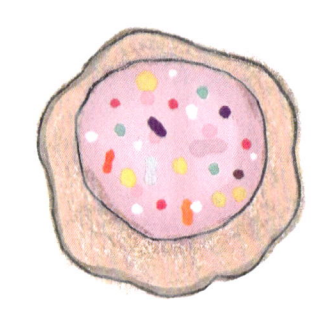

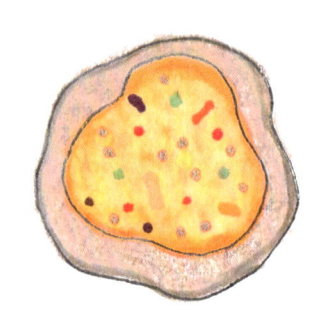

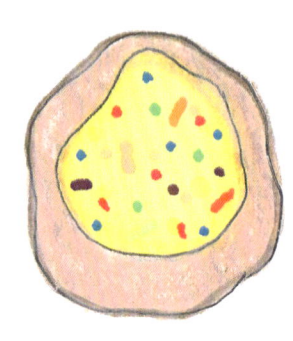

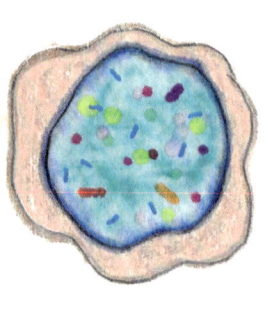

At the end of the week his house looked like it belonged with the rest of the houses in Tangle Town. More importantly, Mr. G. had the warm support of friends, and he knew he lived in the very best place on earth, Tangle Town.

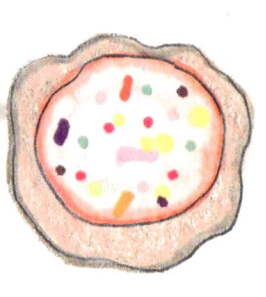

In celebration, Sprinkles passed around her very biggest sugar cookies for everyone to enjoy. She had put even more sprinkles than ever on the cookies because she now knew, without a doubt, that sprinkles were positively magical!

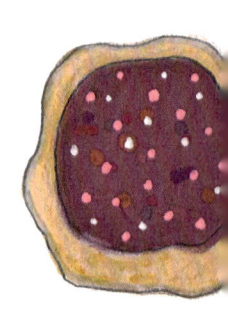

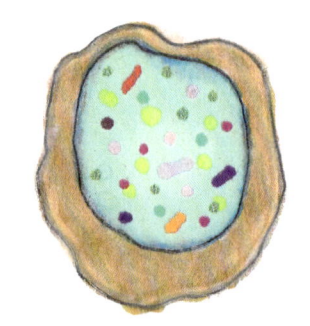

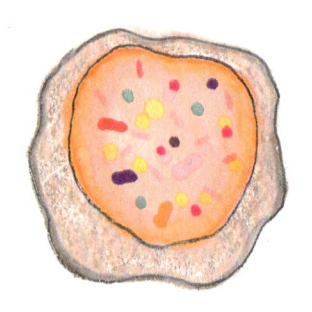

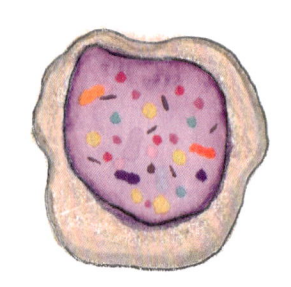

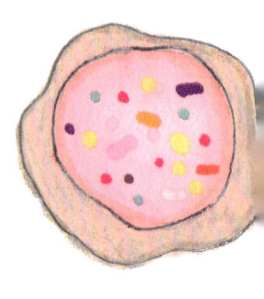

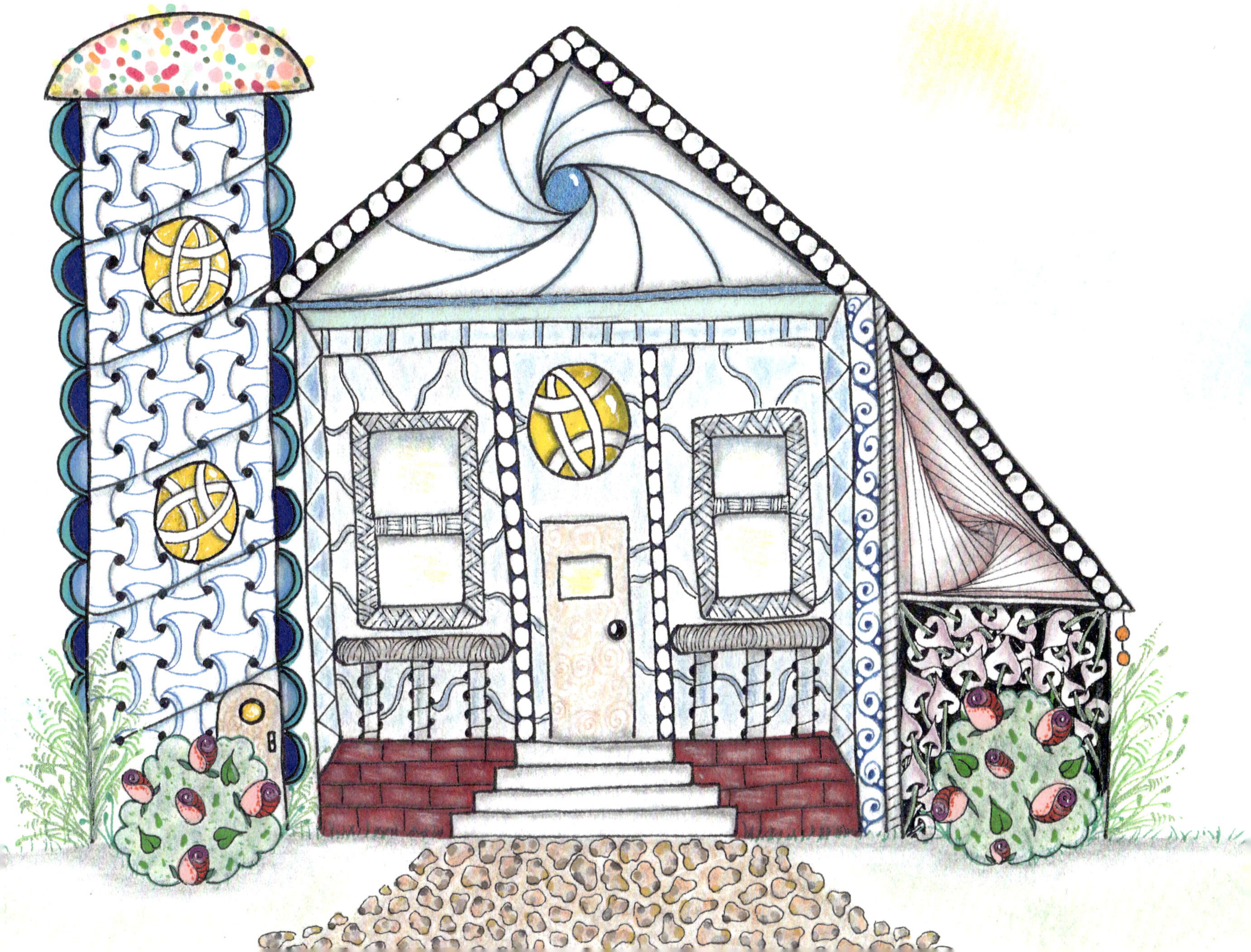

Sprinkles Wonders

Do you know anyone who is shy?

What can you do to help someone who feels left out?

Do you believe in the magic of friendship?

Can you draw and color a house for Mr. Gruff and make it special just for him?

About the Author

Peggy Scott

Peggy Scott is a retired educator, having taught primary grades for 28 years. While teaching, Peggy often piqued her students' interests by writing short poems to integrate into their curriculum. Peggy has previously published a children's book, *Lucky Lizard Little*.

Peggy and her husband, Jay, live in Mesa, Arizona enjoying the desert and the sun's warmth during six winter months. When the heat of the summer comes, they are at home in the cooler air of the White Mountains and the whispering pines of Pinetop, Arizona.

About the Illustrator

Mary Stayner

Mary Stayner, taught elementary school for 35 years. Although retired, Mary enjoys substitute teaching and tutoring. She also enjoys writing and illustrating books. Mary has previously published two books, *Chasin, the Bluebird* and *C.L.A.S.S. (Classroom Language Activities for Special Students)*.

Mary and her husband, Jack, live in the small rural community of Stockton, Illinois. They have two married daughters and eight delightful grandchildren.

In 2018, Mary became a Certified Zentangle® Teacher (CZT), being trained in the Zentangle Method by the founders, Rick Roberts and Maria Thomas. She has shared her love of Zentangle with all ages. If you are interested in learning more about the Zentangle Method go to Zentangle.com. or contact Mary at jmstayner@gmail.com.